D0821528

Weather Update

Clouds

by Maryellen Gregoire

Consultant:
Joseph M. Moran, PhD
Associate Director, Education Program
American Meteorological Society, Washington, D.C.

Mankato, Minnesota

Bridgestone Books are published by Capstone Press,
151 Good Counsel Drive, P.O. Box 669, Mankato, Minnesota 56002.
www.capstonepress.com

Library of Congress Cataloging-in-Publication Data
Gregoire, Maryellen.
     Clouds / by Maryellen Gregoire.
        p. cm.—(Bridgestone books. Weather update)
     Includes bibliographical references and index.
     ISBN 0-7368-3736-1 (hardcover)
     1. Clouds—Juvenile literature. I. Title. II. Series.
QC921.35.G74 2005
551.57'6—dc22   2004010842

Summary: Describes clouds, how they form, and how they affect the weather.

Editorial Credits
Christopher Harbo, editor; Molly Nei, set designer; Wanda Winch, photo researcher;
     Scott Thoms, photo editor

Photo Credits
Airteamimages/Bailey, 20
Capstone Press/Gary Sundermeyer, 4
Corbis/Charles O'Rear, 6; Royalty Free, 1, 10, 14, 18
Dan Delaney Photography, cover (child), back cover
Digital Vision/Jim Reed, 16
Minden Pictures/Foto Natura/Klaus Nigge, 12; Michael & Patricia Fogden, 8
Photodisc, cover (background)

1 2 3 4 5 6 10 09 08 07 06 05

Table of Contents

How Clouds Form

The way clouds form is much like what happens when you breathe out into cold air. Your breath collects water as it passes through your warm mouth or nose. You can't usually see the water in your breath. It is a gas called **water vapor**. When you breathe out into cold air, the water vapor from your breath cools. The vapor forms into tiny droplets that you can see.

Clouds in the sky are formed the same way. Air has water vapor in it. As air cools, clouds form in the sky.

◀ Small clouds form when a person breathes out on a cold winter day.

Condensation

Evaporation

Precipitation

The Water Cycle

Clouds form as part of the water cycle. The sun's heat makes water **evaporate** from oceans, rivers, and lakes. It turns into water vapor and rises into the air. The air gets colder the higher it rises. As the vapor cools, it **condenses** on tiny pieces of dust in the air. The vapor changes into water droplets. Millions of these droplets gather together to form a cloud.

Later, large droplets fall through the cloud. These droplets run into smaller droplets. The droplets join together. They fall to the ground as **precipitation**.

◄ The water cycle moves water from place to place through evaporation, condensation, and precipitation.

Where Are Clouds?

Wet areas have more clouds than dry areas. Clouds often form above rain forests. Deserts have few clouds over them.

Clouds form at different levels in the sky. High clouds are 5 miles (8 kilometers) or more above the ground. Middle clouds are 2 to 4 miles (3.2 to 6.4 kilometers) above the ground. Low clouds are less than 1 mile (1.6 kilometers) above the ground.

Some clouds can cover several levels in the sky. The tallest clouds can be 11 miles (18 kilometers) tall from top to bottom.

◀ Low clouds form above warm, wet rain forests.

Cumulus Clouds

People often draw clouds as puffy white balls. They are drawing **cumulus** clouds. Cumulus means "heap." These clouds look like heaps or piles of cotton in the sky.

Most cumulus clouds have flat gray bottoms. They have puffy white tops. Cumulus clouds usually mean fair weather. They do not bring rain or snow.

◄ Puffy cumulus clouds look like cotton balls floating in the sky.

Stratus Clouds

Stratus means "layer." Stratus clouds look flat. They form low in the sky.

Stratus clouds often bring light rain or drizzle. In cold weather, stratus clouds bring light snow.

◄ Flat stratus clouds form low and cover the sky.

Cirrus Clouds

Cirrus means "wisps of hair." These clouds look like feathery curls.

Cirrus clouds form high in the sky where the air is very cold. They are made of tiny ice crystals.

Cirrus clouds move quickly with the wind. The direction of a cirrus cloud's wisps shows the wind's direction. These clouds mean that warm air is coming.

◄ Cirrus clouds look thin and feathery as they are pushed by the wind.

Nimbus Clouds

Nimbus means "rain." Rain and snow fall from nimbus clouds.

Usually, the words nimbo or nimbus are put together with cumulus or stratus. Cumulonimbus clouds are large puffy thunderstorm clouds. Nimbostratus clouds are dark, layered storm clouds.

Cumulonimbus clouds can grow through all three levels of the sky. They are caused by warm air moving upward.

◀ Nimbus clouds look dark and stormy. Rain is on the way.

Fog

Fog is a kind of stratus cloud. It forms when humid air cools close to the ground. Humid air feels moist, or wet. It holds a lot of water vapor.

Fog usually forms in the morning or evening. It can make things difficult for people to see. Fog often disappears when the air is warmed by the sun.

◀ The road behind a school bus is hard to see through a thick morning fog.

Clouds Made by Airplanes

Airplanes sometimes make clouds. Most planes fly high in the sky. The air is very cold there. Water vapor from the plane's engine changes into ice crystals. A cloud called a **contrail** forms. The word contrail is short for "condensation trail." Contrails sometimes join together to form cirrus clouds.

What kind of clouds are in the sky today? Puffy cumulus clouds mean fair weather is on the way. Thick nimbus clouds may bring rain or snow. Can you predict the weather by watching the clouds?

◀ Bright white contrails form lines behind a jet's engines.

Glossary

cirrus (SIHR-uhss)—high, feathery white cloud

condense (kuhn-DENSS)—to turn from a gas into a liquid

contrail (KON-trayl)—a white, cloudy trail of water that comes out of a jet engine

cumulus (KYOO-muh-luhss)—puffy cloud

evaporate (i-VAP-uh-rate)—to change from a liquid into a gas

nimbus (NIHM-buhss)—storm cloud

precipitation (pri-sip-i-TAY-shuhn)—water that falls from clouds to the earth's surface; precipitation can be rain, hail, sleet, or snow.

stratus (STRAH-tuhss)—layered cloud

water vapor (WAW-tur VAY-pur)—water in gas form; water vapor is one of the many invisible gases in air.

Read More

O'Hare, Ted. *Clouds.* Weather Report. Vero Beach, Fla.: Rourke, 2003.

Sherman, Josepha. *Shapes in the Sky: A Book about Clouds.* Amazing Science. Minneapolis: Picture Window Books, 2004.

Internet Sites

FactHound offers a safe, fun way to find Internet sites related to this book. All of the sites on FactHound have been researched by our staff.

Here's how:
1. Visit *www.facthound.com*
2. Type in this special code **0736837361** for age-appropriate sites. Or enter a search word related to this book for a more general search.
3. Click on the **Fetch It** button.

FactHound will fetch the best sites for you!

Index